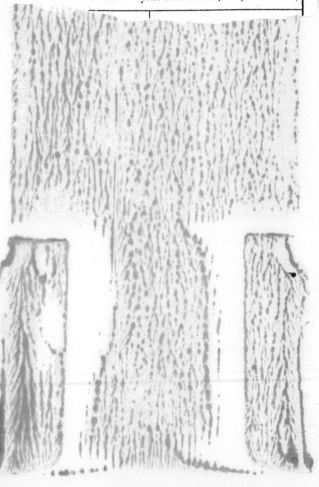

Linguistic Science and the Teaching of English

THE INGLIS LECTURE

1954

Linguistic Science
and the
Teaching of English

HENRY LEE SMITH, Jr.

1966

HARVARD UNIVERSITY PRESS

CAMBRIDGE, MASSACHUSETTS

THIRD PRINTING
LIBRARY OF CONGRESS CATALOG CARD NUMBER 55–11607
PRINTED IN THE UNITED STATES OF AMERICA

THE INGLIS LECTURESHIP

To honor the memory of Alexander Inglis, 1879–1924, his friends and colleagues gave to the Graduate School of Education, Harvard University, a fund for the maintenance of a Lectureship in Secondary Education. To the study of problems in this field Professor Inglis devoted his professional career, leaving as a precious heritage to his co-workers the example of his industry, intellectual integrity, human sympathy, and social vision. It is the purpose of the Lectureship to perpetuate the spirit of his labors and contribute to the solution of problems in the field of his interest. The lectures on this foundation are published annually by the School.

Linguistic Science and the
Teaching of English

I

FROM THE POINT OF VIEW of all of us in the educational world nothing is quite so far-reaching nor so unifying as language. This, you might say, is a natural conclusion to be reached by a linguistic scientist, but only a little reflection is needed to remind us of the overwhelming importance of language in all levels of education, whether we think of teaching language — the native language or a foreign language — or whether we think of the role language plays in mediating all learning. We hear on all sides of the importance of training people to use language effectively, and this realization of the need for developing skilled *communicators* is recognized not only among those who are primarily concerned with the humanities but is reiterated daily by those in charge of engineering schools, medical schools, and law schools, and by leaders in government and industry. To be a truly skilled communicator, for example, is the first requirement of a successful Foreign Service officer, and those who have reached ambassadorial rank are frequently those whose mastery of English is sure and who have acquired control over more than one foreign language.

Along with this mastery and control goes a real insight into our own culture as well as cultures other than our own. For language and culture are inextricably interwoven. Language cannot be taught in a vacuum any more than it is learned in a vacuum. True understanding of the nature and function of language furnishes the best and surest avenue to an understanding of the culture and the way of life of the people who speak it. For in a very real sense, as a man talks, so he thinks and feels. Languages are different because cultures are different, and understanding differences is the greatest task we have confronting us in this unhappy, divided, and shrinking world.

This awareness of the importance of language is evidenced by the emphasis educators have placed on the language arts programs which have become almost universal in American elementary education. Listening and understanding as well as speaking are being stressed along with reading and writing in most of these programs. The advances in the elementary school curriculum have not always been accompanied by understanding or approval, but they are there for all who care to see.

Other great strides have been made by educators and psychologists along the line of understanding the differing aptitudes of children. Though the pendulum at times has seemed to the layman to be swinging erratically between the extremes of progressiveness and "grandfather's way," real progress has been made in what is technically called "learning theory," particularly in the realization that all children who reach the chronological age which entitles them to enter school have not necessarily reached the same level of maturity. This attention to the child as an individual, with his own personality structure, his individual motivations, and with a unique background has been one of the contributions of America to elementary education. It has, in fact, been a very necessary corrective to mass education methods that a democracy like our own is in constant danger of developing. For the conviction that all should have equal opportunities coupled with the mass production of texts, teachers' guides, syllabuses, and training aids can easily lead to a kind of democratic regimentation which leaves little scope for the individual child whose very inability to fit the pattern of the moment might be the best indication of his real superiority. But all this has been said before and said better by those far more qualified to speak of these matters than I am.

But the matter that concerns me this evening is the lack of awareness on the part of our most forward-looking educators of the strides that have been made by linguistic science in the last decades, and the extent to which this progress in the field of analyzing and describing the structure of languages can be applied to the very core of the language-arts program in the elementary grades and the education concerning language and carried on through language in the secondary school. For the science of linguistics has shown us not only how individual languages are structured, but has furnished invaluable insights into how language functions in all cultures everywhere. How the linguistic system interrelates with the other systems of the culture, reflecting and transmitting the content of these systems, is a field that cries out for systematic treatment on all levels of our education. The awareness of the fact that different languages structure experience in different ways, and hence present a different picture of the world to their various speakers, bids fair to open new avenues to the understanding of differences between peoples.

But these considerations would take us too far afield if they were pursued further, though I shall return to this theme from time to time. The particular matter which concerns us here is to explore specific ways in which linguistics can help educators in the extremely important job they have in developing persons to function effectively in the world of today. In order to see the areas in which linguistics can be of assistance we first must realize the level upon which the linguistic scientist operates. This level may be termed the "culturological" level. That is, the linguistic scientist is primarily a cultural anthropologist. The cultural anthropologist is concerned with the way the systematized, patterned, configured events, values, attitudes, and assumptions which we call cul-

ture are *structured*, *interrelated*, and *transmitted*.
All culture must be learned, and the different
cultures learned by the various aggregations of
human beings on this earth is what sets groups
off as different from one another. Now the
psychologist is interested in the individual per
se; the individual within a culture. He is interested, on the one hand, in the similarities
all individual human beings display in common, and on the other, with the differences
which set each individual off from every other
individual. The culturologist and the psychologist, then, can be seen as asking different
questions about the same phenomena. Both
approaches are valid; indeed both approaches
are essential, if vast areas of the utmost importance are to be systematically and fruit-
fully explored. But the time has now come for
the two approaches to be integrated. This is
not just *interdisciplinary* coöperation, it is
inter-level coöperation, a truly different di-
mension.

The linguistic scientist is primarily concerned
with the most important component of one of
the ten basic systems which compose all cultures — language. As can be inferred from

what I have said before, language is in many ways the most important of all cultural systems, for without it the rest of culture and human societies as we know them would be impossible. The possibilities that lie in a truly integrated science of human behavior will never be fully realized until more investigators and observers are systematically aware of the nature and functioning of language. As an example, we will concentrate here on bringing into awareness some facts about the structure of our own language and see some of the implications this awareness has for the teaching of English and the language arts. These implications, and the applications that can grow from their realization, stretch from the teaching of reading in the elementary grades through the secondary school and beyond. They would inevitably lead to a change of emphasis in our teacher-training programs; in short they could imply no less than a revolution in American education.

The first thing that strikes the linguistic scientist when he sees how the language-arts curriculum is set up and administered is that even our best and most forward-looking educators seem to be operating on the assumption

that since the child can't read when he comes
to school, that he must be taught his language.
This is an understandable result of the universal confusion shared by all literate peoples
everywhere — the confusion between language
and writing. The reason for this universal confusion is not hard to find. We learned our
language — all of us — out of awareness. We
learned it thoroughly and we learned it at a
very early age. We can't remember very much
before we had learned to talk well enough to
reinforce our experiences through language.
From many points of view, the learning of
the complex systems through which human
communication goes on — language, kinesics
(or gestures and motions), and vocalizations
(the phenomena generally referred to as "tone
of voice") — is the greatest intellectual achieve-
ment any of us ever makes. And yet these
systems are thoroughly learned and internalized by all physiologically normal human
beings in all cultures at about five and a half
years of age! Individuals learn the systems at
different rates and in different orders, but from
the point of view of the culturologist, the important fact is that about 98 per cent of all our

species are in full control of the *structure* of their group's communication systems at about the same age. This is of extreme importance both as a demonstration of what has been termed "the psychic unity of mankind" and as clear indication that all languages as structured systems must be of about the same order of difficulty, simplicity or complexity. It helps point out the fact that all languages do the job that languages must do just about as well — or as badly — as all others. It makes us realize that the underlying patterns that compose language are the important part of this marvelous system and that once these are internalized, vocabulary items are easy to add, and are added rapidly, as the individual's experience in his culture increases. But probably most important of all from the point of view of a rapport between educator, psychologist, and linguistic scientist is the realization that though language may be considered "the vehicle of thought" and "the means of communicating ideas," "thought" and "ideas" depend in a very real way on the nature and structure of the "vehicle." A real awareness of language and of how languages function

and interrelate with the rest of culture leads
us away from the naïve assumption that
"thought" and "ideas" are universal and
can be "put into words" by all languages in
much the same way. Nothing could be further
from the truth! For the different ways in which
languages structure experience, the obligatory
categories into which the flux of experience is
forced, make speakers of different languages
see the world and relationships in the world
of experience in quite amazingly different ways.
In truth, thought is largely the product of the
language we speak; and logic is for us speakers
of Indo-European languages quite different
from the logic of speakers of Hopi or Chinese
or Eskimo. In fact, since logic is an extrapola-
tion of the basic categories inherent in linguistic
structure, one language is just as "logical" or
"illogical" as any other.

The whole complex we have been speaking
of can be stated as one of the central problems
which is seen differently by linguist and psychologist — the problem of meaning in relation to
language. The educational psychologists have
made tremendous strides in showing that learning and meaning — or meaningful learning —

go hand in hand. The individual — child or adult — learns in context. The normal person's experience is not atomized or fragmented; it is integrated. Realization of this has led to a redesigning and reëmphasizing of the content of what is learned in reference to the matrix in which it is presented. The new methods of teaching arithmetic are an excellent example of this trend, and it has been the principal rationale for the present methods employed in reading. Reading, in this view, has often been defined as "getting meaning from the printed page," and materials are designed and graded with this object primarily and uppermost in mind.

But the linguist, though fully in agreement with the end, has some criticism to make of the means employed. For he as a culturologist has had to focus his attention on the system qua system in order to see how the "vehicle" is put together to carry the "thought." The thought, then, is the meaning of what is communicated between those speaking a common language and participating in a common culture. In order to describe the system that language is, the linguist has had to exclude during this particular stage of his investigation all considerations of "meaning" in the usual sense of the word. This kind of meaning I am going to call "referential meaning" and contrast it with "differential meaning" — the kind of meaning employed by linguists and other culturologists in the analysis and description of all cultural systems.

Differential meaning is simply a statement from a person who has been brought up according to a particular culture to the effect that one cultural event or component of a cultural system is the same as or different from another event. If you ask a fellow American, for example, whether *pin* is the same as *bin* you are likely to get one of two responses: "Oh, no, *pin* is something you use to stick things together, and *bin* is a place where you store coal or grain"; or, "No, one begins with a *p* and the other begins with a *b*." The first answer is phrased in terms of referential meaning and the second in terms of differential meaning. *Pin* and *bin* are not the same word, first because they contain different "isolates" of the sound structure of English — they begin with different initial sounds. Secondly, all who know English and participate in Western culture also know that this basic difference then can be seen to be tied directly to different items in the material systems of our culture — the words mean different things, refer to different things in our cultural milieu.

Now it is the linguist's job to analyze and describe the contrasting components of the structure of language on ascending levels of complexity. Then, with the "vehicle" so described, we can see how language enables us to talk about the different events in the world around us. Language, like all cultural systems, can be seen to be composed of isolates, sets, and patterns — or sounds, words, and constructions, to oversimplify. The way the sounds group into forms and words and the way these in turn pattern into constructions and sentences must be ascertained and stated through the use of differential meaning only; for if referential meaning is resorted to, we immediately open the door to all the other systems of the culture and can never state the structure of the system we are endeavoring to describe and analyze in its own terms. Only when language has been described as a unique cultural system in terms of its own isolates, sets, and patterns can we be on safe ground in seeing how it relates to the other systems of the culture similarly described.

The relationship between language and writing, which we have already stated as universally a cause of confusion, is a prime example of the necessity of analyzing systems in and of themselves before attempting to handle their interrelationships. The way the two systems are handled in the teaching of reading, coupled with the educational psychologist's understandable emphasis on "getting meaning from the printed page," also furnishes our best example of how the different but complementary approaches of linguist and psychologist can combine to place the teaching of reading on a far firmer basis than that which now is employed. For up to now, the linguist who sees reading primarily as a systematic approach to the relationship between sound and letter has not understood or been understood by the reading pedagogue who sees reading as a means to arrive at referential meaning through the printed page. The linguist is appalled by the educator's lack of even the most basic facts about language in general or the English language in particular. The educator is chilled by the mechanical and lifeless approach the linguist seems to bring to reading, which his experience has shown him to be an educational process of primary importance in the child's development rather than simply a mere skill or tool. The reactions of each are understandable, but in the light of the knowledge we now possess, the failure to work together can no longer be condoned.

For the educator is right; reading is far more than just a skill. But the linguist is right; lack of systematic knowledge about the relationship between the system that is language and the derived symbolic system that is writing makes the end the educator and linguist both seek far more difficult to attain. English is written through an alphabet of twenty-six letters which bear a basic patterned relationship to the sounds of the language. The alphabetic principle underlying our writing system must be learned by the individual if he is ever to read in *any* sense of the word. Our modern methods have thrown out "phonics," an old, out-dated, and misleading approach to the alphabetic principle, and substituted for it the learning of words and phrases as wholes. At first blush, to the linguist who sees language as an ascending hierarchy of complexity from sound to word to construction, this seems to be a mistaken doctrine. But here again the educator is right — individuals learn to differentiate sets and patterns before they learn to differentiate isolates. Language itself is so learned and its derived system, writing, is so learned. But sooner or later the isolates must be differentiated or no new sets or patterns can be handled. So again the linguist is right — unless the child is taught at the proper time to see the systematic relationship between sound and letter, his facility in "attacking" new words is meager or lacking entirely. For the linguist again sees "reading" more as an ability to relate sound patterns to letter patterns, whether the individual knows the referential meaning of the item or not. For once the word is "mechanically" read, the context furnishes generous clues to the referential meaning, or the child can ask what the word means. But if the child cannot read the word "mechanically," not much is being accomplished, and it makes little difference whether he knows what the printed or written word means.

The process is further complicated by the fact that our writing system, like all writing systems, is neither complete nor consistent. Some writing systems like those used to represent Turkish, Finnish, and Czech are more consistent than those in use for English or French, but they too are woefully incomplete when it comes to representing all that is in the structure of the language. So the teacher of reading has to be aware of the complete sound system of the language and know first systematically the consistencies that are present in the writing system as well as the inconsistencies. Secondly, the teacher must know the important parts of the structure of the language that are not represented at all in the writing system as well as those which are very sketchily and incompletely represented. These we will take up in just a moment.

But to sum up this part of the discussion, we must remember that writing is a derived and secondary system; that language is primary. Language is a systematization and symbolization of experience; writing is a symbolization — more or less inconsistent and incomplete — of language. Writing is thus a symbolization of a symbolization, and by and large a reminding system to the native speaker of something someone has said or could say in the language. In alphabetic writing systems, sounds are represented by letters; letters do not "have sounds," as all our present reading series state. The child does not have to learn to talk when he comes to school; if he is physiologically normal he is in full control of the structure of his language and all the other communication systems, though his vocabulary is obviously limited by his experience. A good reading readiness program can and should bring the isolates of the sound system into awareness in preparation for a systematic teaching of the relationship of sound to letter, but the school does not have to teach the structure of the native language. Authorities like Betts and Gray seem to be aware of this, and Betts states as the basic requirement of a reading teacher that "she should be keenly aware of the different basic sounds of the English language."* But upon further perusal of Betts'

* Emmett A. Betts, *The ABC Language Arts Bulletin*, vol. II, no. 2, p. 2 (American Book Company, 1949).

Bulletins, the linguist is alternately amused and shocked by the presentation of the "sounds" in relation to their representation in the writing system.

As I have said before, the central confusion has been one between language and writing, mainly owing to the fact that language and the other communication systems are learned early, thoroughly, and out of awareness. It is the linguist's job to bring to the educator the knowledge now in our possession of the *structure* of language — to bring systematically into awareness what the basic sounds, forms, and patterns really are. In doing so, the linguist must also emphasize two things — the relationship between language and writing and the difference in style level between the spoken standard usage of educated people and the various levels of style in the written language, all the way from a note to the milkman to a sonnet by Milton. For as everyone knows, many students entering our schools not only have to be taught to read and write, but they have to be taught standard spoken English. But the difference between substandard and standard spoken English is of a different order than the difference between standard spoken English and the various levels of written or literary English. Most of our grammars are based on an incomplete analysis of the written language, a traditional analysis handed down through the Greeks and Romans and based upon referential meaning criteria. Thus on the level of the elementary school we have basically a confusion between language and writing to combat; in the secondary school, we have this plus a confusion between language as spoken and language as written. On both levels, we have the language work presented from a traditional and prescientific point of view, though vast strides have been made in the direction of educating a whole person — an individual in his own right.

II

In order to see how unaware we traditionally educated people really are of the structure of our language and how much we are confused between the system that is *language* and the derived system that is *writing* we can use no better illustration than the English vowels.

Ask any linguistically naïve but literate speaker of English, "How many vowels are there in English?" and you will get the reply, "Five, *a, e, i, o,* and *u,* and sometimes *y* and *w.*" But only a moment's reflection will make us realize that if we mean by "vowels" vowel sounds rather than vowel letters, there are obviously many more. But how many more? Any speaker can quickly arrive at six contrasts of *short* or *simple* vowels, as for example in the words *pit, pet, pat, put, putt,* and *pot.* Immediately the inconsistency of our writing system is revealed when we notice that *put* and *putt* — words with contrasting vowel sounds — are spelled with the same vowel letter. True, we do add an extra *t* in the word having to do with golf, and this might be a very useful convention in signaling that the vowel letter preceding stands for a different vowel sound, were we always to follow the practice. But we don't, as for example in *but* which rhymes with *putt* but isn't spelled with the extra *t.* It is not hard to see what the foreigner means when he says, "English isn't such a hard language as far as the grammar goes, it's just such a hard language to pronounce." Here he, also being con-

fused between language and writing, is telling
us of our inconsistent and incomplete spelling
system.

So we obviously have at least six short or
simple contrasting vowel sounds in the over-all
pattern of English. But how many more are
there? There is not space here to go into detail
concerning the rigorous process of analysis that
linguists go through in arriving at their statements in answer to that question, but we can
at least try to show the kind of arrangement
that linguists use in seeing the relationships
between the structure points of the vocalic
part of the sound-systems of languages. Speaking in very simple terms, linguists classify the
vowels of languages according to the use made
of the tongue and lips in relation to the mouth
cavity. Thus a vowel pronounced with the
front part of the tongue raised high and almost
touching the ridge behind the upper teeth or
the upper teeth themselves, is called a "high
front vowel." If the lips are spread the vowel
is designated "unrounded"; if the lips are
pursed, the vowel is classified as "rounded."
Likewise a vowel sound uttered with the *back*
of the tongue raised and under muscular tension

is called a "back vowel"; and, depending again upon how the lips are used, "rounded" or "unrounded." For example, the vowel sound in French *titre* or *machine* is a high, front, unrounded vowel; the vowel sound in French *rue* or *tu* is a high, front, rounded vowel. And again the vowel in French *tout* or *boue* is a high, back, rounded vowel. A vowel as in English *but* or *putt* is designated as "mid, central, unrounded," and the vowels in English *put* and *pat* are designated respectively as "high, back, rounded" (though the rounding is slight) and "low, front, unrounded." A chart of the English short, or simple, vowels we have already mentioned will be helpful.

	Front	Central	Back
High	p*i*t		p*u*t
Mid	p*e*t	p*u*tt b*u*t	
Low	p*a*t	p*o*t	

FIGURE I

We notice that in our chart there are three blank boxes with no exemplifying words. A

little more digging and we find that speakers
of English from various dialect regions furnish
us examples of vowels in these areas. For instance, the adverb *just* as in "Just as I came
in" or "Just as he got there" is pronounced
by most speakers from all dialect regions with
a high, central, vowel. The word used here does
not rhyme with *gist* or with *jest* or with *just* (as
said in the phrase "the *just* man"). We have
no symbol for this vowel in our writing system,
so I will use an *i* with a little bar through it
to represent it, ɨ. This vowel occurs very frequently in all varieties of English in stressed
as well as unstressed positions and you will frequently hear it, for example, in the words
children, *this*, and *which*. It is the vowel heard
in the substandard form for the pronoun *you*,
often misspelled "youse," but frequently occurring in the gossip columns spelled "yiz" or
"yez," as in "I thought I told yiz to come."
On the other hand, it is heard in the speech of
Eastern Seaboard dowagers in such a sentence
as, "We're having my *s*ister for d*i*nner," where
again the vowels are not the same as heard in
pit or *bit*, but pronounced with the tongue's
highest position nearer the center of the mouth
rather than nearer the front.

For those of us who distinguish the weak or unstressed form of the pronouns *him* and *them* or who distinguish the possessive of *Rosa* from the plural of *rose*, it is this high, central vowel we employ. For example, "I told'im to come" is contrasted with "I told'em to come" in many dialects by the use of the high, front, vowel as in *bit* or *pit* for the first pronoun and the high, central vowel for the second. And in "Rosa's roses," many speakers will use the mid, central vowel in the possessive of the girl's name and the high, central vowel in the plural ending.

One of the important things to remember in speaking about vowels in English is that not all speakers of the standard language are going to use the same vowels in the same words. It is this different selection, which can be correlated with geographical regions and with position in the social "scale," that helps us to "locate" people by their speech. Carrying this idea further, we can readily see an excellent example of regional difference in the pronunciation of words like *pot*, *lot*, *not*, etc. Most persons from the area of coastal New England will pronounce these words not with a low,

central vowel but a low, back vowel, slightly
rounded. This vowel, but pronounced with
more tenseness of the aural musculature, is
also the vowel used by most British speakers
in these words. It is also very frequently heard
in the speech of Americans from the central
and western parts of the country in such words
as *sorry*, *orange*, and *forest*. In my own dialect
this vowel is relatively rare; I find it in *one* of
my pronunciations of words like "alcohol" and
"Nujol." The symbol I will use for this vowel
is ɔ, a *c* turned backwards and frequently referred to as "open *o*."

We have now identified eight vowels in the
over-all pattern, and because of the few vowel
letters we have to represent them, and in order
to be consistent, I am going to suggest the
following symbolization: *i* as in *pit*, *e* as in
pet, *æ* as in *pat*, ɨ as in "jist," ə as in *putt* and
but, *a* as in *pot* (outside of New England), *u* as
in *put* and *look*, and ɔ as in *pot*, and *lot* in New
England and Great Britain. But we still have
one box on our chart with no examples to
illustrate it. This is the box we would read
"mid, back vowel." It so happens that this
vowel is also extremely common in New Eng-

land. It has in fact frequently been referred to as the New England "short *o*." It is the vowel we hear in the typical "Down Easter's" pronunciation in "I'm gonna be home the whole day," or "I'll put on my coat and go down the road." Here *whole* and *home*, *coat* and *road* do not rhyme with *hull* and *hum* and *cut* and *rud*, though to non-New England speakers this is often the impression. In my own speech, I have this vowel regularly only in "gonna," which is a very frequently occurring pronunciation of this "contraction." Many speakers, however, use ə, the vowel in *but* or *cut*, in the form spelled "gonna," and many others use the high, central vowel, ɨ.

	Front	Central	Back
High	*i* pit	ɨ "jist"	*u* put
Mid	*e* pet	ə putt	*o* "gonna" home (N. E.)
Low	æ pat	*a* pot	ɔ pot (N. E.) sorry (C. and W. U. S.)

FIGURE 2

We have now filled out our chart and placed
our symbols where they belong. But we all
know this is not the whole story of the vowel
sounds in the over-all pattern of English.
What about the so-called long vowels and
diphthongs? Further rigorous analysis of the
speech of persons all over the English-speak-
ing world leads us to the conclusion that
English — like the other Germanic languages
— has a vowel system that can be described
as consisting of simple or short vowels and
what are called "complex nuclei." Complex
nuclei are of three types. First are those composed of any one of the simple vowels followed
by a *glide* to a *higher* and *fronter* tongue position.
Second, we have the simple vowel followed by
a *glide* to a *higher* and *backer* tongue position,
and, third, we have any one of the simple vowels
followed by a *glide* to a more *central* tongue
position. These glides are termed "semivowels,"
because they pattern like consonants, on the
one hand, but fill out the vowel nuclei on the
other. They are the sounds we familiarly represent with the letters *y*, *w*, and *h* as heard in
such words as *ye*, *woo*, and *hah*.

In *ye* and *woo* and *hah* we have excellent

examples of our semivowels *y*, *w*, and *h* used
in both initial and final positions, that is, both
preceding and following a simple vowel. For
if we both listen to and feel what goes on inside
our mouths when we say, for example, *ye*, we
will notice that we start in a very high, front
position and drop to a slightly higher occurrence
of the vowel in *pit* and then return by gliding
to a higher and fronter position. *Ye*, then, is
composed of three segments, *y*, *i*, *y*. Similarly
yay is composed of semivowel *y* followed by
the vowel in *pet*, followed by a return to a
higher and fronter position — *y*, *e*, *y*. By the
same analysis, *woo* is heard to be composed of
a very high, back, fully rounded sound followed
by a slightly higher variety of the simple vowel
in *put*, followed by a return, through gliding,
back to the very high, very rounded sound.
Again we have three segments — *w*, *u*, *w*.
Similarly, *woe* would be *w*, *o*, *w*, and *wow*,
w, *a*, *w*, or *w*, *æ*, *w*.

This analysis of simple vowels plus the semivowels *y* and *w* allows us to handle twenty-
seven vocalic syllable nuclei in English — the
nine simple vowels already taken up, and each
of these followed by *y* and *w*. Examples of all

occurrences of complex nuclei with *y* and *w*
follow, first with *y:*

> *iy* as in *be, me, see, keep, eat.*
>
> *ey* as in *day, bay, pay, gate.*
>
> *æy* as in certain Southern pronunciations of
> *I, July, half.*
>
> *iy* as in Philadelphia and other central dia-
> lects for *me, see, be.*
>
> *əy* as in *first* and *bird* as heard quite typi-
> cally in certain New York City and
> Southern coastal dialects (quite often
> spelled "foist," "boid," in dialect stories
> and comic strips).
>
> *ay* as in *I, my, sigh, might,* in Northern and
> Western speech.
>
> *uy* as in *push* in certain Southern and
> Western dialects.
>
> *oy* as in *joy, boy, Hoyt.*
>
> *ɔy* as in *time, life,* in northern Eastern Sea-
> board dialects and in Ireland.

With *w:*

> *iw* as in *new, few, too, food,* in certain speak-
> ers in the northern Middle West (in-
> stead of the usual *uw*).

ew as in the extreme Southern coastal (Tidewater Virginia) pronunciation of *house, out, about* (often erroneously rendered as "hoose" and "oot" in dialect stories). This is also heard in the extreme form of the "British accent" in such words as *oh, no,* and *go.*

æw as in *how, now, cow, out, around* in most standard speakers, though variations too tense and too nasalized are frowned on by elocution and speech teachers in favor of a nucleus consisting of *aw.*

iw as in *food, moon, spoon* in most central dialects, in contrast to the Northern and Western structuring with *uw.*

əw as in *go, no, so, note,* particularly in Eastern Central dialects (Philadelphia) and as in many British dialects, in contrast with a structuring of *ow.*

aw as in *house, out, about, around, cow, now,* in Northern and Western speech (see *æw* above).

uw as in *food, moon, spoon,* in Northern and Western speech (see *iw, iw* above).

ow as in *go, so, no, boat,* in most of the United States (see *ew* and *əw* above).

ɔw as in the pronunciation of "you all" as a one-syllable utterance in many Southern dialects.

Now for a quick rundown on the complex nuclei with *h*. The *h*, we remember, represents a glide to the center from one of our simple vowel positions. In *hah*, we note that the initial sound has some friction noise along with it, and it starts off without the vocal cords vibrating (or, to use the technical term, "voiceless"). The sound represented by the final *h*, however, is accompanied by no friction voice and is "voiced" all the way through. We have all learned to associate the friction noise, which characterizes *initial h*'s in English, with the letter symbol *h*, and so it comes as a slight shock to see the symbol used to represent the semivowel glide to the center after a simple vowel. In other words, *hah*, *ah*, *pa*, and *ma* all rhyme; all end in *h* though the final *h* is seldom represented in our writing system. It takes only a little careful listening, however, to realize that the initial *h*'s in *he* and in *hot*, though noticeably different in tongue position, are actually starting *nearer the center* of the mouth than the simple vowels that follow them. Even more easily can we notice the gliding to the center from the simple vowel position when *h* follows, as in *idea, poor* and *law*. Examples of the nine simple vowels followed by *h* are:

> *ih* as in *idea, peer. fear* (in New England where "final *r* is not pronounced" the composition of the nuclei with *h* are particularly easy to hear).
>
> *eh* as in *yeah, Mary, bath, past, grass, hand*, though many coastal New Englanders use *ey* in *Mary* and *æh*, or *ah* in *bath, grass*, etc.
>
> *æh* as in *past, grass, bath*, in coastal New England and certain British dialects. Also heard in cultured speech all along the Atlantic Seaboard.
>
> *ih* as in *first, girl, murder* in less privileged speakers of the coastal New England area, where cultured speakers will use *əh*.
>
> *əh* as in *first, girl, murder, fur*. This pronunciation without a noticeable retraction of the tongue (represented by *r*) is the usual one along the North Atlantic Coast and in cultured British speech. It is also heard in Southern coastal dialects,

though it there frequently alternates
with *əy*.

ah as in *calm, balm, ah'd, ma, pa, ah*. Also
heard in *past, last, grass*, by those speakers both in Britain and America who are
said to use "the broad *a*."

uh as in *poor, sure, cure*. Again in those dialect areas where "*r* is not pronounced"
as in coastal New England, the structure
of these nuclei is very easy to hear.

oh as in *law, off, often, saw*, in most of the
Central Atlantic Seaboard dialects and
in many coastal New England dialects.
In Western speech, these words quite
frequently are pronounced with *ɔh*, or
even *ah* (see below).

ɔh as in *law, often, collar, caller*, in many
Northern and Western dialects (see *oh*
above).

This very brief set of examples at least begins
to give us some idea of the complexity of the
structuring of English vowel nuclei. Thirty-six
possible "vowels" in the over-all pattern is
quite a long way from "five vowels — *a, e, i,
o, u*, and sometimes *y* and *w*." The advantage

of the teacher's knowing something about the structuring of the vowel system in the teaching of reading is immediately apparent. In the first place, the preparation of materials which will introduce the child to the printed page through the regularities between the language and its spelling is obvious and has already been mentioned. In the second place, lots of needless confusion and frustration can be avoided if the teacher can be made to understand that *standard* pronunciation varies geographically and that just because Johnny pronounces *bad* as *behd* when the teacher pronounces it *bæhd* doesn't make Johnny "wrong" and the teacher "right." And again, for example, in many standard Southern pronunciations no distinction is made between *e* and *i* before a nasal consonant, so *pen* and *pin* are pronounced to rhyme. To tell standard speakers that this is wrong "because the two words are spelled with two different letters" is as misleading and erroneous as to say that by far the larger majority of educated speakers in the country are "wrong" because they pronounce *merry*, *marry* and *Mary* so that all three words rhyme.

But it is not only in the areas of the vowels

and consonants that our writing system is woefully incomplete and inconsistent. In the handling of the phenomena of *stress* and *intonation* there is an equal or even more striking incompleteness or inconsistency. Let's first take up stress — the structured degrees of relative loudness upon which syllables are uttered. We are all aware that certain syllables are said louder than others in many different contexts. Most noticeably of course this occurs in such contrasting noun-verb pairs as *contract* and *contract*. Good dictionaries give indication of three contrasting degrees of stress, but rigorous analysis of the language shows we have four. These distinctions and the major patterns they form are learned very early and very thoroughly by the child; it seems he is in control of this part of the system of the language by the time he is two and a half years old. Since these are never systematically treated in school, are never represented in the writing system and are learned out of awareness, the educated adult speaker cannot possibly make any statement

about them to, say, the speaker of a foreign
language. But now let's prove to ourselves
that there *are* four stresses and that we've all
learned to react to their patterned occurrences.
Let's take the same three words and notice
how with different stress arrangements they
can be made to *refer* to three different things
in our experience. We'll number them 1, 2,
and 3.

    1. LIGHT HOUSE KEEPER

    2. LIGHT HOUSE KEEPER

    3. LIGHT HOUSE KEEPER

Now in number 1, if we read it so it means "a
person who keeps a lighthouse," we notice that
light is said with the loudest stress, *keep-* is
said next loudest, *-er* is said weakest and *house*
is said not so loud as *keep-* but louder than *-er*.
We will now symbolize and name these four
stresses. The loudest, *primary*, we will symbolize
by an acute accent ($\prime$); the next loudest, *secondary*, by a circumflex accent ($\wedge$); the third loudest, *tertiary*, by a grave accent ($\backslash$); and the
least loud, *weak*, by a breve accent ($\smile$). We

could call the stress degrees by any other names or symbolize them in any desired way just so long as we realize that we are dealing with four significant structure-points in the sound-system of English.

Number 1, then, would be marked:

1. LÍGHT HÒUSE KÊEPĔR,

and immediately we can hear the different arrangement of stresses that accompany these same words to make the whole mean "a person who does light-housekeeping." Number 2 would then be:

2. LÌGHT HÓUSE KÈEPĔR,

and the contrast between this and number 3 is achieved by saying the first word, *light*, not on tertiary stress but on secondary —

3. LÊIGHT HÓUSE KÈEPĔR.

Now, when I ask what the last group of three words means in contradistinction to the other two, you tell me "a housekeeper who doesn't weigh very much." This demonstration establishes the fact that English has four stresses,

40

by the h

what an

in Englis

adjectiva

most fre

seen, by

ceding a

But th

we can l

of prim

a unit

keeper, I

listen to

primary

New ro

as in ou

arrangem

words to

house ke

This b

the stru

I think

with lan

and begins to make us aware of how a very slight variation in loudness can be extremely important in the way our language works. Other examples, for instance, of the contrast between secondary and tertiary stresses can be heard in such a sentence as "Long Island is a long island" or "A New Yorker is not a new Yorker."

Immediately it becomes apparent that an item under secondary stress which precedes an item under primary stress is of *secondary syntactic rank* to the primary-stressed item; or, to put it in more conventional terms, this order and stress arrangement signals that the first item *modifies* the second. But note here no recourse to referential meaning is required. Perfectly automatically I can say that *light* in *light housekeeper* is of secondary rank to *house keeper*, and if I want to talk about a "light-housekeeper" who doesn't weigh very much, I can put *light* in front of "light-house-keeper" with the result LIGHT LIGHT HOUSE KEEPER. The real structural signals received by the hearer in determining "what goes with what and how" is to a large extent dependent in English on order and stress patterns. The adjectival-nominal relationship in English is most frequently signaled, as we have just seen, by an item under secondary stress preceding an item under primary stress.

But there are other patterns of stresses that we can look at systematically. An arrangement of primary followed by tertiary stress signals a unit grouping or "construct" as in *house-keeper, light-house, make-up, black bird*, and *to listen to*. Similarly a tertiary followed by a primary signals a construct as in *Long Island, New Yorker, make up, light-housekeeper*. Also as in our number 1 example above, an over-all arrangement of primary and secondary holds words together to form a construct as in *light-house keeper, elevator-operator*.

This basic and fundamental knowledge about the structure of English is of vast importance, I think we will all agree, for those concerned with language from elementary reading through the entire educational system. Not to be aware of this is often to teach stilted reading in the elementary grades — a kind of rhythm that often blurs the relationships between the items which the child has long ago learned, but out of awareness. The ease with which a child can be made to grasp regular and systematic grammatical relationships later on if he has these facts brought to his attention is astounding, and this can be done from the sixth grade on. Knowing these facts about the structure of his own language is of infinite value in his later attempts at mastering a foreign language, which may structure in a deceptively similar way or may lack a stress system for words entirely, as in the case of French. We may well take a moment to describe the similarities and differences in the operation of stress between German and English. In the first place, German has four levels of stress as does English, and they may be named and symbolized in the same way. Further, German forms many constructs under stress patterns similar to English,

as in the case of primary and tertiary (compare
White House and *Bahnhof*), and as in the case
of primary and secondary (compare *light-house
keeper* and *Sturm bann Führer*). But in the case
of the other two arrangements — tertiary and
primary, and secondary and primary — the
situation is exactly reversed in the two languages. For here, German puts tertiary stress
over an adjective and uses secondary stress
with primary stress to signal a unit construct.
Compare the difference in the stresses in the
following examples:

    The *New Yorker* is a new magazine.

    Die *Neue Zeitung* ist eine neue Zeitung

    (The newspaper *Neue Zeitung* is a new

    newspaper).

A projection of our English stress patterns
on German with a tertiary for a secondary
and a secondary for a tertiary just doesn't make
sense to the speaker of German, any more than
reversing the secondary and tertiary stresses
in *Long Island is a long island* — to get *Long
Island is a long island* — would make sense to

us. But since neither the traditionally educated speaker of either German or English is systematically aware of the stresses and their distributions in either language, they can't tell the other what the difficulty is. Here obviously the linguist can be of great assistance.

But the importance of this matter of being aware of stress obviously doesn't stop at helping us in the proper pronunciation of a foreign language. As I have pointed out previously, the stress patterns and the order of items are the very blood and bone of our grammar. Let me develop here for a moment how important it is for us to know the structural signals if we are ever going to be able to get a realistic picture of how the language actually works. We are all fully aware of the philosophically based, referential-meaning based, definitions of our so-called "parts of speech." "A noun is the name of a person, place, or thing," for example, is solely based in referential meaning. If you already know the language and how it structures experience, the definition finally can mean something to you. But even so, endless hours of classroom time can be consumed in such discussions as those I can remember from my own school days about whether or not "beauty" was a "thing." But the linguist would define his "parts of speech" in terms of "inflectional endings" or "grammatical suffixes." Thus a "noun" is a word (or construct) that can be inflected for plural and possessive, or to put it more simply: "All words that take a plural ending or a possessive ending are going to be called *nouns*." Then you can say that all nouns refer to persons or places or "things" in the culture outside the language. But it is a dangerous mixing of levels to put the cart before the horse.

By the same token, linguists would say that there are at the maximum four "parts of speech" in English — that is four inflected word-classes. These are *nouns; verbs*, inflected at least for past tense; *pronouns*, inflected for subject and object cases and with two possessives; and the class of words that are compared, like *slow, slower, slowest.* Now this last group are called both *adjectives* and *adverbs* in traditional treatments of English grammar and though they are defined in terms of modifying something else, as we have seen, modifying means little unless order, stress, and other structural signals are taken into account. I would prefer to call these compared words "adjunctives" and then note that adjunctives can function adjectivally if they precede a noun and are under secondary stress, as in *slow horse.* Adjunctives function adverbially when they follow a verb and are under primary stress, as in "He drove *slower.*" By this treatment we get out of the morass of "adjective used adverbially" or "inflected adverb" and all of the other confusions that the traditional treatments lead us into, based as they are on referential meaning and with no systematic use of the stress phenomena in the language.

Using order and stress criteria we can also arrive at statements about our "syntactic parts of speech" — those items that are not inflected

in the language. For example you can divide
the group of uninflected words like *up, out, to,
through, in* (which have been called prepositions
and adverbs) into two classes, depending upon
their occurrence in relation to inflected words
and what stresses fall on them. So a preposition
will be one of these words that precedes a noun
(or nominal construct) and bears weak or tertiary stress — *thròugh thĕ woóds, ĭn thĕ hoúse,*
etc. Also we will call these words prepositions
when they immediately follow one of the forms
of a verb (under primary stress) and are themselves under tertiary stress — *tŏ lísten tò, tŏ
swím ìn,* etc. But when one of these words immediately follows a verb bearing tertiary or
secondary stress and occurs itself under primary
stress, we will call it an adverbial — *"He càme
tó," "He dròve ín."*

Time does not permit our going more thoroughly into this whole matter, but I hope I
have indicated that an awareness of structural
signals and a rigorous analysis of the structure
of language on levels of ascending complexity

can furnish us with neat and unequivocal statements of how the language actually works. We then have a firm basis from which to proceed into the consideration of the whole problem of referential meaning.

III

So far, we have been mainly considering, very rapidly and far from thoroughly, the building-blocks of our language, the basic isolates and sets. I would like to turn now to the consideration of one of the basic patterns, the *intonation pattern*, which encloses, so to speak, the words and constructs and gives us the clues and signals as to the sentence. Now, much ink has been spilled as to what a sentence is and what it should be. Again here referential meaning has been the criterion rather than a structural analysis based on differential meaning. The sentence has been defined in various ways but most generally from the point of view that it "must express a complete thought." The linguist, who leaves the analysis of the thought content or referential meaning to a later stage, is concerned with the structural signals the speakers of the language use to indicate that the *sentence pattern* of the language has been completed. Here once more we have to concern ourselves with the building-blocks the language uses in its system or structure from the simplest components to the most complex of its patterns. Let us bear in mind that this complexity, startling as it may seem from one point of view, is in the possession of the physiologically normal individual before he is six years old.

The area we want to consider now, then, is the area of intonation. Here our language uses the pitch of the voice, and has abstracted, so to speak, four significant levels. These relative significant pitch levels are part of the sound-structure of English in a way analogous to the four significant levels of relative loudness or stress. We will symbolize them by the numbers 1, 2, 3, 4 — with 1 standing for the lowest level and 4 for the highest. In order to bring into awareness how the pitch levels operate we can take an ordinary sentence: "He's going to Paris." Said as a statement of fact, we all would agree that the highest level of pitch falls on the syllable that bears the primary stress, the first syllable of *Paris*. As we are going to see, this is pitch 3. The sentence starts on pitch 2, as do most of our sentences, and pitch 2 continues over the whole stretch of syllables until the primary stress on *Paris*, when it rises to 3. After that syllable, we notice a sharp drop in pitch, a drop in fact to pitch 1. Our sentence could be marked then as follows.

$$\overset{2}{\text{He's going to}} \overset{3\nearrow 1}{\text{Paris.}}$$

Now if I should ask you how you would describe the event that takes place after the fall in pitch from level 3 to level 1, you would most likely say something like, "Well, you just stop talking," or "You sort of fade off into silence." This is, in fact, a very accurate description of just what happens. The machines in the acoustic physics laboratories show us that there is a gradual diminution of intensity until silence is reached. This is a real structural signal in languages of our type, and I'm going to symbolize it by #, and call it by its technical name — "double-cross juncture." Now a juncture is a signal of transition in a language; junctures are the ways we signal to each other how we get from one stretch of utterance into another or how we complete utterances and start others. The double-cross juncture is an example of what we call a "terminal juncture," because it signals the end of an "intonation pattern." The intonation pattern of our sentence above would be transcribed 231 #, since intonation patterns are composed of pitches and terminal junctures. In our writing system the period as a punctuation mark is the very over-worked symbol we use, but not consistently, to symbolize the double-cross juncture.

Let's look at another sentence now. Suppose speaker B in our conversation was not quite sure he'd heard the first speaker, A, correctly, and was surprised by what he thought he did hear. He might well say, "He's going to Paris?" Here we note that the sentence starts on pitch 2, as in the previous sentence, rises to pitch 3 at the same point, but stays on 3 throughout the whole word *Paris*, and then rises in pitch slightly at the end. Is this rise an example of pitch 4? In order to answer this question, let's take another sentence, one this time from a third speaker, C, who heard perfectly what A had said but asked the following question, "Why's he going to Paris?" in such a way as to imply "and not London or Cairo or Berlin." C's pitch on the primary stressed syllable of *Paris* is now an example of pitch 4, and you can easily hear the greater height in pitch between the 4 and the rise heard from 3 at the end of B's question. C's pitch then falls rapidly to level 1 and trails off into silence as A's did, another example of #. The rise at the end of B's question, then, is an example of another terminal juncture, one characterized by a *rise* in pitch, but not up to the level of the next highest significant pitch point. This we will symbolize by a double bar, ‖, and call it "double-bar juncture."

We can now transcribe our whole interchange as follows:

A. $\overset{2}{\text{He}}$'s going to $\overset{3}{\text{P}}\nearrow\overset{1}{\text{aris}}$ #

B. $\overset{2}{\text{He}}$'s going to $\overset{3}{\text{P}}\nearrow\overset{3}{\text{aris}}$ ‖

C. $\overset{2}{\text{Wh}}$y's he going to $\overset{4}{\text{P}}\nearrow\overset{1}{\text{aris}}$ #

We now have here examples of all four of our significant pitch levels (or pitch phonemes) and two of our terminal junctures. We also have examples of the following intonation patterns — 231 #, 233 ‖, 241 #.

But we still have another juncture that ends an intonation pattern. Let's listen to the following sentence.

What're we having for dinner, Mother? If this is said in the normal, ordinary way by a properly dutiful son or daughter, we would hear it start on pitch 2 with a rise to 3 on the stressed syllable of *dinner*. The pitch then falls to 2, *not* to 1, at the point where the writing system puts a comma, and we would describe the event that then takes place as a "slight pause, or break." Then we hear pitch 2 again on the primary stress on *Mother* and a continuation on 2 over the weak-stressed syllable and finally the slight rise in pitch we symbolize by ‖. Now the "slight break or pause," which is characterized neither by a fading off nor by a rise in pitch is another terminal juncture, in contrast to the other two. This one is termed "single-bar juncture" and is symbolized by |. We would transcribe our sentence, then, as follows:

$$\overset{2}{\text{What're}}\ \text{we having for}\ \overset{3}{\text{dín}}\overset{2}{\text{ner}}\ |\ \overset{2}{\text{Mó}}\overset{2}{\text{ther}}\ \|$$

and we now have examples of two more intonation patterns, 232 | and (2)22 ‖.

It's important for us to realize that pitch and stress are independent systems in English, though interdependent. That is, most frequently the primary stress coincides with pitches 3 or 4, but there are numerous occasions when this is not the case. Let's take our sentence above and use the intonation pattern (1)11 # instead of the pattern (2)22 ‖ on *Mother*, as follows:

What're we having for dinner | Mother #

Here, when the primary stress occurs with pitch 1, and this continues throughout the word *Mother*, terminating with a #, we get the impression that the speaker is not being nearly so polite to his mother as our culture says is right and proper. If we go further and use a pitch 1 on the stressed syllable of *dinner*, continuing on pitch 1 throughout the remainder of the sentence, the effect is even more pronounced, and we get the impression that the speaker does not highly regard his mother as a person or as a cook.

What're we having for dinner | Mother #

This gives us another intonation pattern, 211 |.

The important thing to bear in mind here is that intonation patterns have no encapsulated referential meaning, but that their selection plus the words, the vocal qualifiers, the other systematic "tone of voice" phenomena, and the kinesics (gestures and motions) taken together furnish the totality which then can be related to the other systems of the culture.

We who speak English and who have been enculturated as Americans are obviously extremely sensitive to the difference in meaning we have learned to associate with the selection of different intonation patterns in various contexts. It is the totality of the interrelation of the various components of language and of the other communication systems which is the basis for referential meaning. So the altering of one isolate in an intonation pattern — a pitch phoneme or a terminal juncture — can register significantly on the hearer who has learned the structure of the communication systems and their relationship to the other cultural systems.

To illustrate this, let's examine another series of sentences. A asks B how he likes his new boss. B pauses noticeably before replying and says

$$\overset{2}{\text{H}}\text{e has a }\overset{3}{\text{v}}\overset{\nearrow}{\text{ery pleasant}}\overset{2}{\text{ }}\mid \overset{2}{\text{ }}\overset{3}{\text{pe}}\text{rson}\overset{\nearrow}{\text{ality}}\overset{2}{\text{ }}\#$$

Here note that B does not fall to pitch 1 at the end of his reply but remains on 2 followed by #, giving us another intonation pattern —

232 #. In the actual speech situation from which this example was recorded, A laughed when he heard B's reply because the inference was obvious — the only *good* thing the boss had to recommend him was his outward pleasantness; everything else he had was, to say the least, disqualifying. After laughing, A asked B, "Did you put a period or a semicolon after that?" and B replied, "I'm afraid I put a period after it." If A and B had learned our analysis in school — where in my opinion they should have — and had been familiar with our system of symbolization, A would have said, "I'm sure I heard you right, but I'm asking did you end your intonation pattern with a *double cross* or a *double bar?*" Because if B had used a 232 ‖ intonation pattern, as noted below, the inference would have been, "He's a very nice person *but* . . . I don't like the way he talks to his wife at the bridge table," or some other relatively minor pejorative statement.

He has a very pleasant | personality ‖

But if B had replied by using a 231# intonation

pattern on *personality*, the statement would
have been entirely complimentary.

He has a very pleasant | personality #

Thus a change of only one pitch or juncture
phoneme can bring about a change of intonation pattern which, when used with the same
words, can alter the entire message from one
of an extremely complimentary nature, to a
mildly disqualifying one all the way to what
amounts to an insult, though couched in "diplo-
matic words." We begin to see what we mean
when we say, "It isn't so much what he said
as how he said it," or "It wasn't his words I
objected to, but his tone of voice." But tone of
voice is not found merely in the intonation
patterns, it also is found in other systems,
particularly in the one termed "vocal qualifiers," such as drawl, overloudness, rasp, over-
fast tempo, and so on, which, like kinesics, go
along *with* language in order to form the total
context of communication. We haven't time to
consider these in detail, but it would interest
some of you to hear, I'm sure, that many psy-

chiatrists are now very much interested in the systematization that linguists have been able to bring to this extremely important area of man's out-of-awareness behavior, since valuable insights concerning the cues passed between patient and therapist in the psychiatric interview can now be clearly and explicitly stated. The correlation between the use and distortion of any or all of the communication systems and various mental disturbances is also beginning to be systematically studied. The importance of this area in cross-cultural relations is also obvious. To think we have "translated" from our language to another when we have taken care of the *word level only* is a very dangerous and naïve mistake.

But I'd like to return for a moment to our consideration of what a sentence is. A sentence on one level — the phonological — is a stretch of speech bounded by an intonation pattern ending in # or ‖. A phonological nonsentence is one ending in a single bar (|). A complete syntactic sentence is one having a subject and a predicate, but the linguist doesn't have to define the subject as "the thing talked about" and get into the kind of confusion I remember in such sentences as "John gave Mary the book," as compared with "The book was given Mary by John" or "Mary was given the book by John." Any noun or nominal construct which precedes a verb or verbal construct in normal order is by definition the subject of the sentence. The predicate is the part containing the verb and any other nominal or adjunctival material following — called the "complement." The various orders of the sentence components can be as systematically stated, frequently signaled by internal junctures. The whole thing is easily reduced to systematic statements which can be taught once and for all, since the statements have to do with structural reality and not with any philosophical considerations of referential meaning.

But once so stated, what a firm foundation there is for a really sound exposition of the artistry of our great literary stylists! How much easier it would be for us to grasp fully and completely the whole matter of acceptable levels of style in the spoken language as related to the various interactive situations in which we find ourselves. And finally, how much easier to control the structure of a foreign language so presented in contrast to the structure of our own language, similarly taught and learned.

Again in conclusion, the linguist is not setting himself up as a person or as a member of a group to criticize adversely the work of the professional educator. Rather he like all informed laymen applauds from the sidelines the great progress that has been made by our school people. But he does believe that a rapport between linguist, anthropologist, psychologist, and educator can lead to a strengthening of understanding, a realistic appraisal of success and failure that can make our progress in the last twenty-five years — great as it has been — seem paltry in comparison to what can be done. We are, I feel, at the dawn of a new era, and I believe it is a group like the one here tonight that can do the most toward bringing the results of this interdisciplinary coöperation into the actuality of the school room.

THE INGLIS LECTURES

THE BURTON LECTURES

THE INGLIS AND BURTON LECTURES